GW01238875

Explorers
1450-1550

DINAH STARKEY

Contents

Introduction

The United Kingdom is in the **continent** of Europe. Two other continents are joined on to Europe. They are Asia and Africa. You can get to Asia and Africa by going overland but you must cross the Atlantic Ocean to reach South or North America.

But hundreds of years ago Europeans knew nothing of America and most of the rest of the world. A lot of early maps were very inaccurate, like the one below.

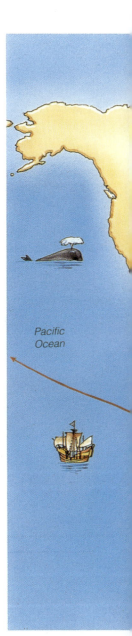

Pacific Ocean

▲ Early Europeans drew maps of the world the way they thought it was described in the Bible. Jerusalem was the most important city in the Bible, so it is marked as a big red dot in the centre of this 13th-century map.

Early explorers wanted to find a sea route to Asia. You could travel there by land, but it was a long, hard journey. The Turks would not let you travel over the lands they ruled.

This book tells the story of some of the explorers who began to discover what the world really looked like. Some of their journeys have been drawn on a modern map that shows the real shapes of the continents. But the early explorers did not have maps like these. They often sailed where no European had gone before. If an astronaut ever lands on Mars, he or she will know more about that planet than the first explorers knew about our world.

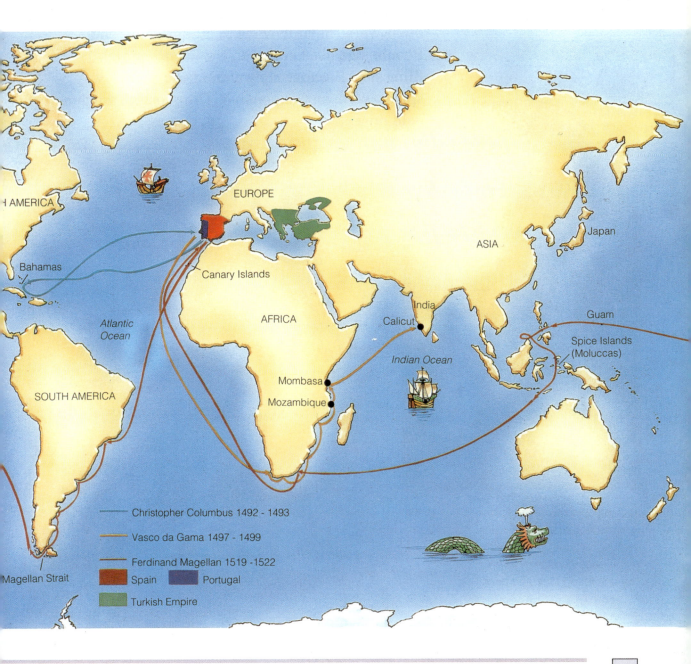

H AMERICA

EUROPE

ASIA

Japan

Bahamas

Canary Islands

India

Guam

Atlantic Ocean

AFRICA

Calicut

Spice Islands (Moluccas)

Indian Ocean

Mombasa

SOUTH AMERICA

Mozambique

Magellan Strait

— Christopher Columbus 1492 - 1493

— Vasco da Gama 1497 - 1499

— Ferdinand Magellan 1519 -1522

Spain   Portugal

Turkish Empire

Maps and Marvels

Spices

The story begins in 1350. In those days, the people of Europe had only visited parts of Asia and Africa.

Asia was rich. It was the land of silks and **spices**.

Rich people used spices to make their food taste better. Spices could help disguise the nasty taste of meat that was starting to rot. Drying or pickling meat were the only ways to stop it going bad. People also used spices to try to cure many illnesses. Because they came from so far away, spices were very expensive. They cost as much as gold dust.

▲ Can you pick out the rich French nobleman in this 15th-century picture? He is feasting with friends and family while servants bring food and drink.

▶ Some of the spices the early explorers hoped to find.

nutmeg

cinnamon

mace

cloves

ginger

pepper

Africa

Africa was a mystery. Very few travellers had ever been there. Nobody really knew what it was like. There were all sorts of tales about the people who lived there. A 14th-**century** English travel book said:

> On one island there are men as big as giants. They have only one eye and that is in the middle of their forehead. They eat raw meat and fish.
>
> In that land are men that have only one foot and it is so big ... it will cover his body against the heat of the sun.

▼ These are some of the strange people who were supposed to live in the lands Europeans had not yet visited. On the right of the map on page 2 you can see some more strange creatures.

People usually travelled by land. Boats stayed close to the coast because sailors could easily get lost once they lost sight of land.

People once thought the world was flat and that ships would fall off its edge. Educated people who could read believed the world was round, but they did not know how big it was. They could only guess at what lay beyond the great oceans. One writer thought that:

The first place in the East is Paradise. The Tree of Life grows here, surrounded by a wall of fire.

▶ By 1489, mapmakers had begun to realise what the world really looked like. Which parts of the map do you think are accurate? Use an atlas to help you.

a How many differences can you see between the feast on page 4 and your own meals at home?

a Use an atlas to find an overland way to Africa. Find one to Asia. What problems might you have on your journey? What sort of lands should you avoid?

b Pretend you are writing in the 14th century. Make up some really good travellers' tales. Use the picture on page 5 to help you.

c Which spices do we use today? Look at the picture on page 4. Use a recipe book to find a list. Why do you think spices are so much cheaper now than they were then?

The Spice Lands

Marco Polo was a traveller who had been overland to Asia. He wrote a book, *The Travels of Marco Polo*, in the early 14th century which told of the riches of the East. He wrote of a fabulous island called 'Cipangu', where a huge palace had roofs and floors made of solid gold. He never visited the island but we now call it Japan. He travelled all over Asia and he described the lands where spices grow. He wrote about a nearby island:

> The island [of Java] grows pepper, nutmeg, cloves and other valuable spices. There is much gold. The people hunt for diamonds in the rivers. There are valleys full of diamonds.

The book made people want to go to Asia, to buy spices and silks. But it was a long and dangerous journey, and the Turks would not let Europeans cross their lands to reach Asia.

▼ Marco Polo gathering spices in India.

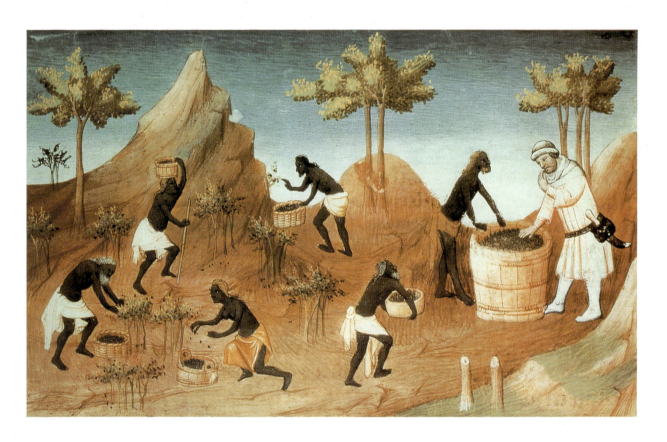

At the same time, Europeans began reading a book that they had ignored for hundreds of years. It was called *A Guide to Geography* by Ptolemy, a Greek, and it was over a thousand years old. Although Ptolemy lived in ancient times, he knew more about the world than the people of Marco Polo's day. He knew the world was round, but he thought it was much smaller than it really is. This map was copied from Ptolemy's book.

These two books got sailors and merchants thinking. The overland route to Asia was too difficult. What they wanted was a sea route.

Prince Henry of Portugal made up his mind to find one. He sent ships out to sail down the coast of Africa, looking for a way through into the Indian Ocean.

▼ Ptolemy drew lines on his map. Lines of longitude ran down the map and showed how far east or west a place was. Lines of latitude ran across the map and showed how far north or south a place was. We still use this idea on modern maps.

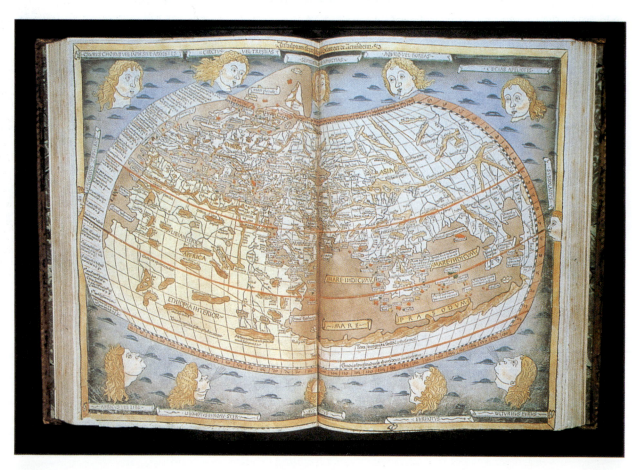

Monsters and terrors of the unknown

The early sailors were afraid that if they sailed past Cape Bojador, they would come to the Green Sea of Darkness and be swallowed up forever by storms and whirlwinds and sea-serpents. The sea monsters below come from a book. Its writer said of one:

This monster of the sea can sink even a large ship by sucking in water and then blowing it out again in clouds through holes in its forehead.

Eleven times Prince Henry sent his ships out to explore the coast of Africa. Eleven times the captains turned back at Cape Bojador, too frightened to go further. Eventually, one captain took his ship past the cape.

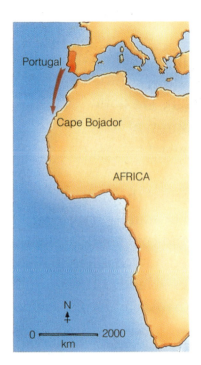

▲ The winds and currents by Cape Bojador would drive a ship southwards. Sailors knew the sun got hotter as they went south. They were afraid of reaching a place where the sea boiled and the sun roasted them alive.

▲ These monsters come from a book printed in 1550, over 100 years after a European had sailed past Cape Bojador. It was many years before sailors lost their fear of imaginary sea monsters.

From then on, the Portuguese slowly worked their way down the west coast. They took note of everything they saw. When a ship returned from a journey, the captain reported back to Prince Henry's team of mapmakers. One captain described Senegal.

All the coast is covered with fine, green trees. In the market people brought cotton, cloth, oil and wooden bowls. The wild beasts are lions, lionesses, and leopards in great numbers.

By 1488, the Portuguese had reached the very southern tip of Africa. They had gradually improved their ships until they were fast and could sail far out into the oceans. They had learned how to navigate out of sight of land and how to map new lands. It was their skill which made possible the Age of Exploration.

▶ Busy Portuguese shipyards in Lisbon in the 16th century.

Slaves

But there was a cruel side to their voyages, too. The Portuguese made slaves of some Africans they found. They captured them and carried them back to Portugal to sell. The Portuguese captains grew rich on slavery.

▶ Explorers capturing Africans for slaves.

a How well do you know the shapes of the continents? Draw a map without looking at an atlas. Check it with an atlas. Which bits did you get right?

b Look at Ptolemy's world map on page 8. Then look at a world map in an atlas. Which bits did he get right? Which parts did he know best?

c Write a report from one of Prince Henry's captains, describing all the sights you have seen on your journey down the coast of Africa. Make drawings of any rare animals you see.

d Use the map on pages 2 and 3 to plan a sea route to Cipangu from the United Kingdom.

Life at Sea

Explorers used two main types of ships. A **caravel** was a small but strong ship that sailed well. A **carrack** was bigger and held more cargo but did not sail as well as a caravel. Some ships had square sails, which worked best if the wind blew from behind. Triangular sails, called 'lateen sails', did not need a wind to blow in the same direction as a ship was sailing.

Life was hard on board ship. Sailors spent all their time out on deck. They cooked there, they ate there and they slept there at night, on a pile of cloth or sacks. Only the officers had cabins.

A sailor who fell asleep on watch (on look out) was whipped or ducked in the sea. Seamen who disobeyed the captain and made trouble were hanged.

▼ This painting shows how ships could ride up and down huge storm waves. It also gives us an idea of how unpleasant life could be on a caravel or a carrack.

Food and drink

Fresh food was a problem because it soon went bad. The explorer Christopher Columbus wrote in his **log** (a diary) in 1492:

> Today we loaded dried meat and salted fish and some fruits. We will have to eat the fruit quickly because it will spoil if the journey takes three weeks. We will load the biscuits tomorrow.

On long journeys food became inedible and water became undrinkable. Sometimes they ran out altogether. This happened on Ferdinand Magellan's voyage round the world.

> We ate biscuit which was a powder swarming with worms. It smelt of rats. We drank yellow water which had gone bad for many days. We ate sawdust from the boards. Rats sold for half a gold piece and even then we could not get them.

▶ Loading 16th-century ships with stores. The small ships probably stayed close to the shore or sailed on rivers.

Lack of fruit and vegetables caused a horrible disease called **scurvy**. This is what scurvy did to Vasco da Gama when he sailed to India.

It rotted my gums, which were turning black and blue and growing over my teeth. I cut away the dead flesh and rinsed my mouth and teeth with urine, rubbing them very hard. Many of our people died of scurvy every day.

Sailors were afraid to go on these long voyages. Some captains had to use criminals from the prisons. They agreed to sail in return for their freedom if they got back alive. Even when they got on board, they were still afraid. They could go for weeks on end without a glimpse of land.

▶ The man at the top of this African ivory carving stands in the crow's nest. High at the top of the ship's mast, he kept a look out for land. Why do you think this was so important for sailors?

Sailors knew that if the food and water ran out, they would die. Sometimes they plotted together to kill the captain and turn back. This happened to Columbus in 1492.

▼ These are some of the things sailors ate on voyages. Dried fish kept for months. It had to be soaked in water before you cooked it. Sailors drank a lot of wine because water often turned green and went bad.

I am told by a few trusted men (and there aren't very many of those) that if I keep on sailing outwards, the plan is to throw me over the side and then say I fell overboard.

dried cod
ship's biscuits
cheese
salted meat
raisins
honeycomb
garlic
chick peas
rice
lentils
almonds

a What kind of food did the sailors eat? Plan what you would take with you on a voyage. How would you store it? Use the picture above to help you with ideas.

b What good things might seamen expect from a voyage of exploration? Make a poster to get them to sign on for your voyage. What can you offer to make them want to come?

a Make a list of food that soon goes bad. Make a list of food that stays good for a long time. How do we stop food going bad nowadays?

Finding the Way

It was easy to get lost in the middle of the ocean. There were no landmarks and maps were inaccurate.

The captain used a **compass** to find the way. He planned where he wanted to go and marked it on a map. This was called charting a course. Then he looked at the compass to find out which way to steer. At night, sailors steered by the Pole Star. They knew that if they headed for the Pole Star, they were going north.

The steersman needed to know the time. So an **hour-glass** (like a big egg timer) ran night and day. There was always a boy on duty to watch it and turn it over when the sand ran out. But on cold nights, the boys sometimes cheated. They would warm it up to make the sand run faster.

▼ This hour-glass was about 15cm high. It took half an hour for the sand to run out.

▶ A captain's compass. One of the points of the compass was specially marked to show north. Can you see which one it is?

Sailors worked out a ship's speed by timing how long it took the length of the ship to pass a motionless piece of floating wood or seaweed. The captain multiplied the distance travelled in one hour by 24 to work out how far he had gone in one day.

Each day the captain worked out where he was. He marked on a map how far the ship had sailed and in what direction. He added up the daily distances travelled to discover how far he had gone since his journey began. This was called **dead reckoning**. On 16 September 1492 Columbus wrote in his log:

I sailed night and day to the west and must have gone about 117 miles.

A captain had to know how far north or south he was. The horizon is where the sky seems to touch the sea or land. As you move north or south the sun and stars appear in different positions above the horizon. The captain measured these positions with an **astrolabe**. Measurements in a book of tables told him how far north or south he was. Only dead reckoning gave the captain an idea of how far east or west he had gone.

▼ Arab astronomers invented the astrolabe to find the positions of stars. But they used it on land. It was very difficult to use on a ship deck tossing in a storm. One sailor held the astrolabe while a second sailor took a sighting on a star or the sun.

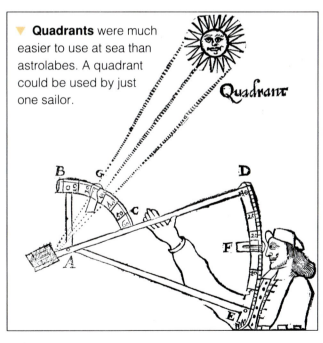

▼ **Quadrants** were much easier to use at sea than astrolabes. A quadrant could be used by just one sailor.

Quadrant

None of these navigation aids was very accurate. A tiny mistake or storms and currents could take a ship hundreds of kilometres off course.

A captain often used clues to guess his position. Columbus wrote in his log on 4 October 1492:

More than 40 petrels [a sea bird] came to the ship. A boy hit one of them with a stone. A frigate bird came to the ship and a white bird that looked like a gull. So many birds are a sure sign that we are near land.

Thursday 11 October

I saw several signs of land... a green reed was found floating near the ship... those on the *Nina* saw a little stick covered with barnacles.

▼ Taking measurements on land was much more accurate than from a wave-tossed ship's deck. Can you see what is marked on the round table?

a Plot a course with a compass around the school. Write down the number of steps you take in each compass direction. Ask a friend to follow your course.

b Use a watch to time one turn of an egg timer. Calculate how long five turns will take. Test to see how long they really take.

c Look at the pictures in this chapter. How did each instrument help sailors to navigate?

Christopher Columbus

Christopher Columbus was born in Genoa (part of Italy today) in about 1451. He dreamed of finding a new sea route to the East Indies, so he could trade in the spices growing there.

His plan was to sail west. He thought he could get to the East by sailing round the world.

But it was a new idea and nobody would back him. For years he tried to persuade King Ferdinand and Queen Isabella of Spain to pay for his voyage. He told them it would make Spain rich and powerful and help spread the Christian religion across the world. Finally, they gave him three ships - the *Nina*, the *Pinta* and the *Santa Maria*.

He left Spain on 3 August 1492 and sailed to the Canary Islands near the African coast. They took on more stores and headed westward across the Atlantic. For weeks there was no sign of land. You can read what happened on the next page.

▲ Christopher Columbus.

◄ A full-sized copy of the *Santa Maria*. The builders of the original *Santa Maria* did not use paper plans, so we are not sure what it really looked like. How many differences can you see between this ship and the model below?

Land! Land!

Christopher Columbus's sailors were frightened because they were so far from home. They had been at sea for over three months since they left Spain. Several times his men thought they could see land. But each time it was a false alarm. Then they really did see an island. This is Christopher Columbus's story of how they first spied land and his first few days on the island. The story is based on what he wrote in his log.

Thursday 11 October 1492

After sunset I told the crew to keep a good look out. I promised a silk jacket to the first man to sight land. He would also get a rich present from the king and queen.

About ten o'clock at night I thought I saw a light to the west. It was like a little candle bobbing up and down.

At two o'clock in the morning a seaman high up in the *Pinta*'s crow's nest cried out, 'Land! Land!' The men on the *Pinta* fired a cannon. It was my signal for sighting land.

At dawn we saw naked people and we went ashore in the ships' boats. We leapt out onto the shore and kneeled down and kissed it. We tearfully thanked God for rewarding us after such a long and strange journey. I raised the royal banner and claimed the island for the king and queen. I gave the island the name San Salvador.

As soon as we had done so, people began to come to the beach. All the people I

saw were young. They are well-built with handsome bodies and very fine faces. They wear their hair short, but they have a long piece at the back which they never cut.

Many of the natives paint their faces black, white and red. They are friendly people. They carry no weapons except small spears, and they have no iron. I showed one my sword and he took hold of it by the blade and cut himself. Their spears are made of cane and they fix a fish tooth, or some other sharp thing, at one end.

This afternoon, the people came swimming out, or paddling boats made out of logs. They brought parrots, balls of cotton, spears, and many other things, including a dry leaf, which they value highly. For these we swapped them little glass beads and bells.

These people would make good servants, for they are quick to learn. I think they can easily be made Christian for they seem to have no religion. God willing, I shall take six of them back to Spain, so that they can learn to speak Spanish.

I have tried very hard to find out if there is any gold here. I have seen a few natives who wear a little piece of gold hanging from a hole made in the nose. I believe that if I go to the south, I will find a king who has lots of gold which he keeps in big containers.

◀ We think Columbus landed on this shore. It is on the tiny island of San Salvador in the Bahamas.

Columbus's mistake

Columbus was sure that he had sailed right round the world and was close to Cipangu (Japan). If you look at the map, you can see why he made this mistake. The world was much bigger than he thought and in fact, he had only got half way round.

He had reached a group of islands called the Bahamas. They are off the coast of America. Columbus believed they were the Indies. He spent about three months sailing from island to island, looking all the time for gold and spices. On 27 October 1492 he wrote:

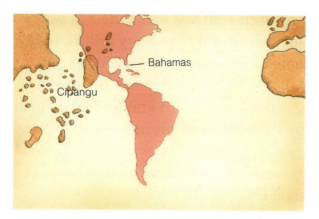

The lands printed in brown on this map are taken from a globe made in 1492. The lands printed in red show the correct position of the American continent. What did the globe maker get wrong?

> I took up the anchor at sunrise and sailed for Cuba. I am told it has gold and pearls. I am sure Cuba is the Indian name for Cipangu.

He returned to Spain in March 1493. Columbus made three more voyages across the Atlantic but he never did discover his mistake. To the end of his life he believed he had found the sea route to Asia.

a Why did Columbus go to the Indies? What was he hoping to find? What did he hope to do?

a Do we know what the *Santa Maria* really looked like? Make a list of evidence that might help.

Vasco da Gama

Vasco da Gama.

Vasco da Gama was the first European to sail to India. He left Lisbon, Portugal's capital, in July 1497 with four ships. They were the latest design and two were specially built for him. His equipment was the best that money could buy. He planned to sail further than any of Prince Henry of Portugal's explorers had already gone. But he did not sail all the way down the west coast of Africa, where there were dangerous currents and storms. Instead, he soon turned west, into the Atlantic. There he hoped to catch strong winds that would drive his ships down to the tip of Africa.

Da Gama took about 140 men with him. Each sailor had a special skill. There were rope-makers, carpenters, sail-makers and blacksmiths.

He took enough stores for three years and he made sure his men had plenty to eat. These were one man's daily rations:

$1\frac{1}{2}$ pounds of biscuit   1 pound of beef or

$2\frac{1}{2}$ pints of water $1\frac{1}{2}$ pounds of pork

$1\frac{1}{4}$ pints of wine   oil and vinegar

Vasco da Gama's plan worked. By Christmas day he had sailed right round Africa's tip and was heading up the east coast. He had already gone further than any other European. On his way up the east African coast, he stopped at Mozambique, a busy trading port. The Arab chieftain was indignant at the cheap gifts da Gama offered him. Instead, he demanded red cloth, but da Gama did not have any. Further up the coast at Mombasa, the local people tried to capture da Gama's ship.

Eventually, da Gama reached Calicut in India, where Arabs and Persians traded between Africa and India. They did not want to trade with da Gama, for they feared the Portuguese would take over their rich trade routes. They even plotted to kill him. Da Gama decided to turn back for home. But many men had died on the long voyage. When he returned to Lisbon in 1499, over half his men were dead, including his brother Paolo. But da Gama was a hero. He had found a sea route to India.

▼ This tapestry shows Vasco da Gama arriving in Calicut. It was woven by a European who had never been to India. He imagined the buildings there would be like the ones he knew.

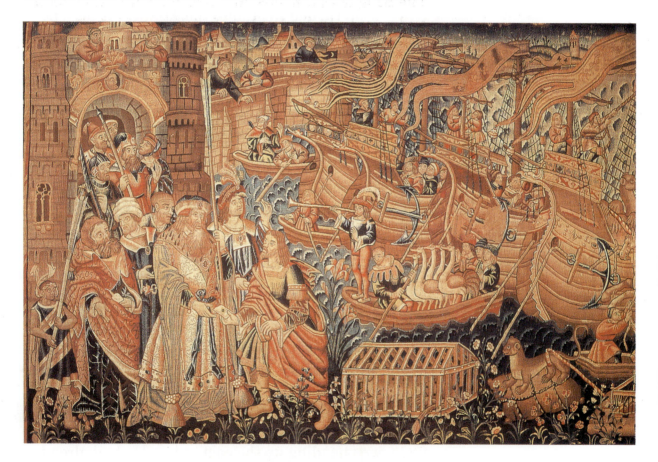

◼ **a** Write a newspaper report about Vasco da Gama's return to Portugal. Interview one of the survivors from his crew.

▲ **a** Draw the route of Vasco da Gama's journey on a map. Can you find the route many ships follow from Europe to India today?

Ferdinand Magellan

Magellan was Portuguese, but he was working for the King of Spain. Like Columbus, he believed he could get to the spice lands by sailing west. He knew Portuguese sailors had begun exploring Brazil and the west coast of South America. Magellan had no idea of just how big South America was. He thought if he followed where the Portuguese had already gone, he could find a **strait**, a way through from the Atlantic to the Pacific.

The King of Spain gave him five old, patched up ships and a crew. In September 1519, they said their prayers and set off. At first, all went well. The little fleet reached South America and stocked up with fresh food:

Potatoes, sweet pineapples - in truth, the most delicious food that can be found - the flesh of tapir, sugar cane and innumerable other things.

▶ Ferdinand Magellan.

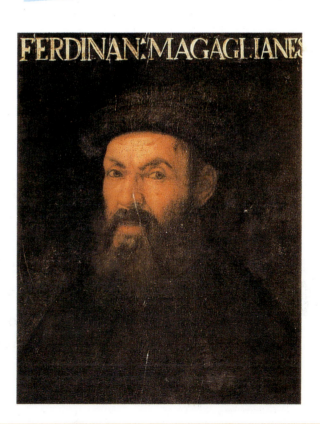

FERDINAN:MAGAGLIANES

But they could not find a strait to let them through from the Atlantic to the Pacific. They went further and further, and the weather grew colder and colder. Winter was coming on and they were running out of food.

The crew **mutinied**. Magellan hanged the leader and continued the search. They found the strait in October 1520. Magellan named it after himself and you can see it on the map today - just above the tip of South America - the Strait of Magellan.

It took 38 days to sail through to the Pacific and then they found themselves sailing for weeks on end with no sign of land. The water was stinking and they were eating rats. One of Magellan's captains deserted and sailed his ship back to Spain.

It was March before they made landfall at Guam. Then they headed for the Moluccas, the Spice Islands. But Magellan never got there. He was killed in a native war in the South Sea Islands and died with a spear through his heart.

▼ The Strait of Magellan is a very narrow passage. Strong currents and high winds could easily drive a ship onto dangerous rocks that would rip a hole in a ship's bottom.

By now three ships remained. One was abandoned. The other two reached the Spice Islands and loaded up spices. One was later wrecked. Only one ship got back to Spain in September 1522. Only 18 men returned - 250 had started. But the *Victoria* was the first ship to sail around the world.

▶ People still grow spices on the Moluccas. These Moluccans are weighing cloves.

◨ **a** Find someone to pay for an expedition to the Spice Islands. Write them a letter explaining how you plan to go, what you hope to find, and what you will need in the way of ships, crew and equipment.

b Draw a carrack or a caravel. Draw as many members of the crew as you can, and write what each one is doing. The last two chapters should give you some ideas.

△ **a** Look at a globe. Can you use it to follow the voyages of Columbus, Magellan and Vasco da Gama?

b Look up the dates of each of the voyages of discovery and chart them on a time line. Do you know anything else that was happening in the world at the same time? Add that to your time line.

The Aztec way of life

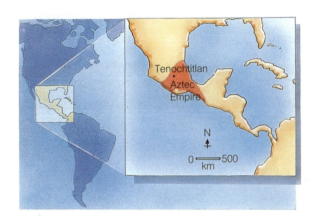

▲ The lands the Aztecs once ruled lie in the thin strip of land between North and South America. We call this part Central America.

Once Columbus and Magellan found a route to America, other Spanish and Portuguese followed. They found that people already lived there. The explorers named them Indians, because they still thought they were near the Indies.

In the part of South America which is now called Mexico, the Spanish came across a new people. These were the Aztecs.

Tenochtitlan, the capital city of the Aztec **Empire**, stood in the middle of a great lake. Three bridges joined it to the mainland.

▶ This painting shows the great Aztec capital in the lake.

▶ Many of the canals around the Aztec capital can still be seen today.

Markets

An Aztec goldsmith at work. Can you see what he is doing? His son, who would follow his father's trade, watches.

This modern painting shows the Aztec market. A smell of roast meat in sauces and honey-toasted seeds tempted shoppers as they gossiped with friends.

The Aztecs could buy all they needed in a huge city market that was open 24 hours a day. Everybody needed **maize** (sweetcorn) to grind into flour to make pancakes called tortillas. Some wanted small hairless dogs to cook and eat. Other stalls sold dried meat or fish, sweet potatoes, yams, tomatoes, avocadoes and fruit such as plums, bananas or pineapples. Craftsmen bought gold and jewels to make the jewellery they sold. There were animal skins, beautiful bird feathers, embroidered clothes or woven sandals. Artists found paper and paint, and women could buy brooms, clay cooking pots, mats, herb medicines or eye-shadow.

Rich people bought slaves to do farming, work in kitchens or entertain their owners with music or dancing. Only the rich could afford tobacco to smoke or cocoa beans to make chocolate for special occasions. A hundred cocoa beans could be exchanged for a woven cloak, for the Aztecs did not use money. A feather cloak cost 100 woven cloaks.

Gods

Beyond the markets lay the palace. The king, Montezuma, lived there with his thousand wives and his courtiers. Nearby stood a tall pyramid with two temples.

The Aztecs had many gods. The Sun God was very important. The Aztecs thought there were once five suns. One by one they died, until only one was left. He needed blood to stay alive. Every day Aztec men, women and children pricked their ears with cactus spines to make them bleed. They offered the blood drops to the god. But the Sun God needed more. So they **sacrificed** slaves or prisoners captured in wars. They cut open the prisoner's chest and took out the heart to offer to the Sun God. They thought that the sacrificed people did not die, but went up to live in happiness with the Sun God. Most people who were sacrificed believed this too, and willingly died to join the Sun God.

▼ An Aztec painting of a human sacrifice. Sometimes as many as 100 people would be sacrificed at a time.

A Spaniard who visited the temple of the Sun God in 1568 described it like this:

> On each altar were two figures like giants... the body was girdled by snakes made of gold and precious stones. The walls were so splashed and encrusted with blood that they were black.

God of the dead

The God of the Dead had a face like a skull. He ruled the underworld and he too liked human sacrifice.

▼ This knife was used for human sacrifices. It was made of black glass from a volcano.

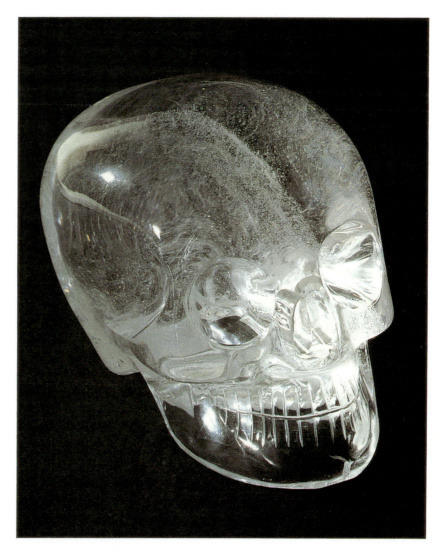

▲ This skull was carved from rock-crystal. Nobody knows what it was used for. Perhaps it was a present to the God of the Dead.

The Aztecs believed the all-powerful gods controlled everything, from the seasons to the result of a game. The gods could be kind or cruel. It partly depended on how the Aztecs behaved and if it was a lucky or unlucky day of the month.

The Plumed Serpent

But there was one kindly god. He was Quetzalcoatl, the Plumed Serpent. Stories told how he gave the Aztecs the gift of corn. He taught them to make music, to grow things and to spin and weave.

But the demons grew jealous of him. They tricked him and drove him away. He sailed away to the east on a raft made of snakes, promising that he would return.

So the Aztecs believed that one day a strange magical visitor would come out of the east. When the first Spaniards came, shining silver in their armour, the Aztecs thought they were the god and his servants, and were afraid of them.

▶ Quetzalcoatl, the Plumed Serpent, was the friend of humans. A beautiful bird with long green tail feathers lives in Central America today. It is called the 'quetzal'.

Festivals

The Aztecs held many festivals to please the gods. Soldiers and women, dressed in beautiful feathered cloaks, danced and sang far into the night. In one ceremony, men tied to ropes flung themselves from the top of a pole to make themselves spin round the pole until they touched the ground.

A favourite board game was 'patolli'. Men gambled at it and prayed to the god of dance and music for luck.

▼ The god watches men play 'patolli'.

▶ An Aztec painting of men getting ready to perform the pole ceremony. Mexicans still perform it today. Each of the four men had to fly round the pole 13 times before reaching ground.

◨ **a** Draw a picture of an Aztec market place. How many different stalls can you think of? Use this chapter, and the pictures on page 29 to help you. Make a list of the different things sold in your local market today.

Education

The Aztecs did not use writing as we do. They had signs for numbers and for the most common words, but apart from that, they used pictures.

An Aztec month had 20 days. Each day had a sign, such as water, rain, wind, eagle or ocelot (a small wild cat), and a number between one and 13. The Aztecs believed some pairs of numbers and signs were lucky and others were unlucky. An Aztec born on 10 Eagle would be strong and brave, but someone born on 1 Ocelot would become a slave.

▶ These are four of the Aztec days. Starting on the left, they are: Ocelot, Eagle, Vulture and Earthquake. The circles above the signs show the number of the day. When 13 was reached, the numbers started again at one.

Growing up

The picture below tells how children should be brought up. At the top, the boy is learning to gather reeds and the girl is learning to grind corn. Can you see what skills the children are learning in the bottom two pictures?

▶ Aztec children learning skills to do the work they will do when they are older. The writing was added by a Spaniard. The blue dots over each child's head are Aztec numbers. They show how old the children are. The round circles are tortillas. They show how much food children will eat.

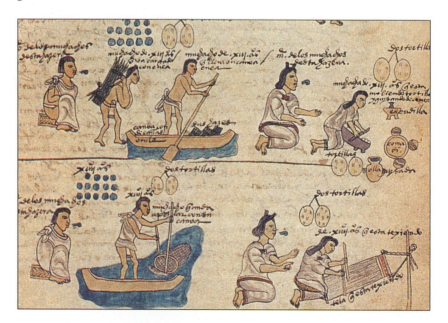

Aztec parents were very strict. If their children were naughty, they held them over a fire of hot peppers, to make their eyes sting. Children were trained to be brave.

▶ What is happening to this child? How old is the child? How many tortillas did the child have to eat?

◑ **a** Some of what we know about the Aztecs comes from the pictures they drew. Some comes from what the Spanish wrote down about them. Which do you think is the best evidence? Why?

◪ **a** Try drawing pictures of the main things that happened to you yesterday. Then write down everything that happened. Ask a friend to decide which tells him or her most.

b Make a chart of the Aztec numbers up to 20. Write our numbers underneath. Draw the numbers and day signs for an Aztec born to be a slave or born to be brave and strong.

The Spanish conquerors

△ Hernando Cortes.

Hernando Cortes had heard of the rich Aztec Empire, and he went there to seek his fortune. Like other Spaniards who came to South America, Cortes also believed he had a duty to stop the Aztecs praying to their own gods and to become Christians instead.

He set sail with 600 soldiers, some guns and 16 horses. When he landed, in 1519, he needed to find a guide who spoke the Aztec language. He chose a clever girl, whom he called Marina, who soon learnt Spanish.

▶ The girl with the long dark hair is Marina. You can see her in every picture the Aztecs drew of Cortes, for she was always by his side to advise him.

The Aztecs feared the Spanish. They thought the strangers came from the east in floating hollow mountains. They carried sticks which spat thunder and lightning and they rode on monsters. One Spaniard wrote:

The Indians thought that the horse and rider were one creature, for they had never seen a horse before.

Quetzalcoatl's return

The armour of these strangers shone silver and their faces were hairy. The Aztecs decided they must be gods. Quetzalcoatl had returned, as he had promised.

The king, Montezuma, sent them presents. He allowed them to enter the capital and gave them rooms in his own palace. But as time passed, the Aztecs realised they were not gods. They were men, and they were greedy for gold. An Aztec said:

They picked up the gold and fingered it like monkeys. Their bodies swell with greed. They hungered like pigs for it.

These two pictures show Montezuma meeting Cortes. One was painted by an Aztec, the other by a Spaniard. Can you see which is which?

Cortes treated the Aztec king well, but when he was called away, another Spanish officer attacked and killed many Aztec lords, so as to steal their gold jewellery. The Aztecs rose up against the Spanish. Montezuma tried to calm them, but his own people killed him.

Sad Night

The Spanish waited for dark and fought their way out of the city. All night long the battle raged. Many died. Spanish and Indian bodies were piled high. The Spanish called it the 'Noche Triste', the Sad Night, for they had lost the battle.

After the battle, Cortes marched away what was left of his army to plan a new attack. But in the city, the Aztecs were dying of a disease called smallpox that they had caught from the Spanish. Because it was new to the Aztecs, it killed thousands of them.

▶ This picture of the 'Sad Night' was drawn by an Aztec. The Aztecs, dressed for battle in feathers and animal masks, attack the Spanish. What differences can you see between the Spanish and Aztec weapons? Who has the best armour? Can you see Marina?

The end of the Aztec Empire

Cortes returned with more men and cannons. He blasted down the walls of the city and entered it. The Aztecs fought to the last but illness and hunger weakened them. In 1521 Cortes took the city and destroyed it. The Aztec Empire was at an end.

CONQVISTA DE MEXICO POR CORTES...&Z.

▲ This Spanish painting shows the destruction of the Aztec capital city.

a Do you think the Spanish were right to fight the Aztecs? Make a list of reasons for and against the Spanish. Talk over your list with a friend.

a Draw a series of pictures to illustrate this story. Try to draw them as if you were an Aztec.

b Look at the two pictures of the meeting of Montezuma and Cortes on page 37. Make a list of all the differences you can see. What is Montezuma thinking, as they meet? What is Cortes thinking? Write down your ideas.

The Spanish Empire

Cortes once asked Montezuma if he had any gold, saying,

Send me some of it, because I and my men have a sickness which can be cured only by gold.

Cortes conquered the Aztecs and made his fortune. Other Spanish soldiers wanted to do the same. They were called **conquistadores**. One of them was Francisco Pizarro.

▼ This modern Mexican picture shows how the Spanish had used the Aztecs and their lands to make themselves rich.

The Inca Empire

High in the Andes mountains, on the west coast of South America, there was once a great empire in the place we now call Peru. It was ruled by the Inca emperor. His people, the Incas, worshipped him as a god.

The Inca kingdom was very rich. It stretched thousands of kilometres. In the capital, Cuzco, stood the Inca's palace and the Temple of the Sun. It was covered with gold sheets. The Incas believed gold was the sweat of the sun and silver the tears of the moon.

The Inca ruled everything. He told his people when to plant or harvest, when to make roads and when to go to war. The Incas built roads and bridges right over the high mountains. The Inca's messengers travelled the roads. Incas had no form of writing, so the runners carried messages in their heads. They also had a knotted string called a 'quipu'. Every knot had a special meaning.

▶ High in the Andes, Machu Picchu is near the Inca capital. The fortress was one of the last Inca strongholds against the Spanish.

In 1530 Pizarro took 180 men and 27 horses to attack the Inca kingdom. When they landed on the coast of Peru, some were afraid and wanted to go back. But Pizarro led the rest into the Andes where the Inca waited, surrounded by his soldiers and courtiers. The Spanish were hopelessly outnumbered. But Pizarro captured the Inca by a trick. He knew that if he held the ruler, he could make all the Incas obey him.

For nine months, Pizarro held Atahualpa, the Inca ruler, prisoner. The Spanish gave orders but pretended they spoke for the Inca. The common people obeyed the Spanish without question.

Atahualpa saw the Spanish greed for gold. He offered to give Pizarro a whole room filled with gold in return for his freedom. He sent out word to his people across the empire. Gold poured in. The Inca people stripped the temples to pay the ransom.

▼ Incas were skilful goldsmiths. Can you see what kind of animal this might be?

When the room was full, Atahualpa asked for his freedom. But Pizarro broke his promise. He put the Inca on trial and condemned him to death. When the king was dead, the Inca Empire ended. There was nobody to tell the people what to do and the Spanish took over. They became the new rulers of Peru.

Treasure for Spain

The Spanish conquistadores stripped Peru and Mexico of their treasure. They melted down the Aztec gold to make plates and cups for their churches. Silver from Peru was made into ingots, great bricks, and sent back to Spain. The heavily loaded treasure ships attracted pirates who tried to capture them. Some were sunk, and to this day divers are still trying to find the wrecks so as to bring up the treasure which is now worth many millions of pounds.

▶ This Spanish plate was made from silver and gold taken from South America.

◗ **a** Why did Pizarro want to conquer the Inca Empire?

◪ **a** List the similarities between the Aztecs and the Incas.

b Look at the painting on page 40. What do you think the artist thought of the Spanish? Make a list of what the Aztecs and the Spanish are doing.

South America Today

The country of the Aztecs is now called Mexico. But you can still see many signs of the times before Cortes. The Aztecs worshipped the God of the Dead and made offerings of bones and skulls. Today, Mexican families celebrate and feast on the Day of the Dead when they happily welcome back the souls of dead relatives. Like people all over the world, Mexicans eat hamburgers and drink Coca Cola, but they also enjoy tortillas and many other dishes the Aztecs ate. In some small villages you may still hear musical instruments like the ones the Aztecs played.

The Spanish also left their mark. They brought with them a new instrument - the guitar. Today, most Mexican bands of musicians include several guitarists.

▼ A stall selling sugar skulls in modern Mexico. Parents buy these skulls for children on the Day of the Dead. On the right of the picture you can see some sugar angels. Do you think they are a sign of the Aztec past or of the Spanish past?

The Spanish also stopped the Indians from sacrificing to their old gods, and built Christian churches where the temples used to stand. Because of the Spanish, most South Americans are now Roman Catholic.

The official language of Mexico and the South American countries once ruled by Spain is Spanish. But hundreds of different languages from before the Spanish conquest are still spoken in different parts of the countries. In Mexico, for example, over 50 different languages are still used. One is 'Nahuatl', the ancient Aztec language.

Mexico and the other countries conquered by Spain now have laws like Spanish laws. Many of the people are half Spanish and half Indian.

▼ Musicians and dancers at a festival held in front of an old Spanish church in Mexico. Where did the instruments originally come from? The Mexicans wear festival costumes. Who are they remembering?

The Spanish changed the countries they invaded for ever. But the invasion changed Europe, too. The Spanish bought back maize, peppers, avocado pears, tomatoes, kidney beans, vanilla, pumpkins, turkeys and chocolate. They also came back with rubber and valuable hardwood such as mahogany from the great South American forests.

▼ These are some of the things that you can find in a supermarket that originally came from South America.

a Did anything good come of the Spanish invasion? What bad things came of it? Have a class debate about the good things and bad things.

a Look at a map of South America. How many places can you find which are named after saints? These were named by the Spanish and Portuguese.

b Next time you go to the supermarket, have a look to see which foods come from South America.

Glossary

astrolabe   An astrolabe measured the position of the stars or sun in the sky.

caravel   A small sailing ship made of wood. A caravel could fit inside the white lines of a modern tennis court.

carrack   A wooden sailing ship slightly bigger than a caravel.

century   A century is a hundred years. We live in the 20th century. The 15th century began in 1400.

compass   A compass has a needle that always points north. It tells you which way you are travelling.

conquistadores   Spanish soldiers who conquered South America.

continent   The earth is divided into five great land areas, the continents of Europe, Asia, Africa, America and Australia.

dead reckoning   Working out how far a ship had travelled by adding up the estimated distances sailed each day.

empire   A group of countries ruled by one person or government.

hour-glass   An instrument that measured time by letting sand run out. Clocks at this time were too unreliable and delicate to use at sea.

log   The captain's diary of all the important things that happened on a ship's journey.

maize   A kind of corn. We call it corn on the cob.

mutiny   A sailors' plot to overthrow their captain.

quadrant   This instrument did a similar job to an astrolabe but was much easier to use at sea.

sacrifice   Something that is offered to a god.

spices   Strong-tasting seeds or bark used to flavour food.

scurvy   An illness you get if you do not get enough vitamin C by eating fresh fruit and vegetables.

strait   A narrow strip of water leading from one sea to another.

Index

Acknowledgements

The publisher would like to thank the following for permission to reproduce material.

Ancient Art and Architecture Collection p10, Ferdinand Anton p36 (left), Bibliothéque Nationale p18, Bodleian Library, Oxford p29, p34, . p35, The Bridgeman Art Library p4 (left), British Library p6, p8, British Museum p31 (left), Comstock Photo Library pp20/21, ET Archive p2, p7, p9, p17 (right), p31 (right), p32, p33 (left and right), p36 (right), p39, p42, Robert Francis, South American Pictures p44, Ian Galloway p41, Giraudon p13, p24, Robert Harding Picture Library p19 (top left),p23, p25, p27, Michael Holford p14, p16 (both), p17 (left), Kunsthistorisches Museum, Wien p12, p43, Rebecca Marvil, Light Sources, Stock p19 (bottom left) Mexicolore p28 (both), p29 (bottom), p33 (inset), p40, Tony Morrison, South American Pictures p45, Science Museum, London p19 (bottom right), Miss LA Strickland p37 (left), Survival Anglia p26, Syndication International p5, p11.